I0763038

CHARTER

OF THE

PEMBERTON AND HIGHTSTOWN RAILROAD CO.

ALSO,

THE AGREEMENT BETWEEN SAID COMPANY

Transportation Library
HE
2791
.P36
H61

AND THE

JOINT COMPANIES;

ALSO, THE ACT OF

RATIFICATION OF SAID AGREEMENT;

AND A

COPY OF THE MORTGAGE

EXECUTED TO SECURE THE BONDS OF THE SAID PEMBERTON AND HIGHTSTOWN RAILROAD COMPANY.

TRENTON, N. J.:
PRINTED AT THE TRUE AMERICAN OFFICE.
1867.

CHARTER

OF THE

PEMBERTON AND HIGHTSTOWN RAILROAD CO.

ALSO,

THE AGREEMENT BETWEEN SAID COMPANY

AND THE

JOINT COMPANIES;

ALSO, THE ACT OF

RATIFICATION OF SAID AGREEMENT;

AND A

COPY OF THE MORTGAGE

EXECUTED TO SECURE THE BONDS OF THE SAID PEMBERTON AND HIGHTSTOWN RAILROAD COMPANY.

TRENTON, N. J.:
PRINTED AT THE TRUE AMERICAN OFFICE.
1867.

CHARTER.

An Act to incorporate the Pemberton and Hightstown Railroad Company.

1. Be it enacted *by the Senate and General Assembly of the State of New Jersey*, That George F. Fort, Samuel Stockton, Rescarrick M. Smith, Benjamin Reed, Nathaniel S. Rue, Gilbert S. Lawrie, Richard H. Conover, John S. Irick, Job H. Gaskill, Joseph K. Hulme, Collin B. Meirs, James S. Giberson, Richard Waln, Harrison G. Wright, and such other persons as may be hereafter associated with them, shall be and are hereby ordained, constituted and declared to be a body politic and corporate, in fact and in name, by the name of "The Pemberton and Hightstown Railroad Company;" and shall be capable of purchasing, holding and conveying any lands, tenements, goods and chattels whatsoever, necessary or expedient for the object of this incorporation. Names of corporators.

2. *And be it enacted*, That the amount of the capital stock of said company shall be five hundred thousand dollars, with liberty to increase the same to one million of dollars, and shall be divided into shares of fifty dollars each, which shall be deemed personal property, and transferable in such manner as the said corporation shall by their by-laws direct. Capital stock.

3. *And be it enacted*, That the above-named persons, or a majority of them, shall be commissioners to open books to receive subscriptions to the capital stock of said corporation, at such time or times, and place or places, as they, or a majority of them, may think proper, giving at least twenty days' Commissioners to open books.

notice of the same in four of the newspapers published in this state; and that, at the time of subscribing, ten per centum shall be paid for each share subscribed for, to the commissioners, or some one of them; and as soon as two hundred thousand dollars of the capital stock shall be subscribed, such commissioners shall give like notice for a meeting of the stockholders, to choose nine directors, a majority of whom shall be residents of this state; and such election shall be made at the time and place appointed, by such of the stockholders as shall attend for that purpose, either in person or by proxy, each share of the capital stock entitling the holder thereof to one vote; and the said above-named persons, or any three of them, shall be inspectors of the first election of directors of the said incorporation, and shall certify, under their hands, the names of those persons duly elected, and deliver over the subscription books and money paid in (deducting all expenses previously incurred,) to the said directors; and the time and place of holding the first meeting of said directors shall be fixed by the persons named in the first section of this act, or a majority of them; and the directors chosen at such meeting, or at the annual election of said corporation, shall, as soon as may be after every election, choose out of their own number a president, who shall be a resident of this state; and in case of the death, resignation, or removal of the president or any director, such vacancy or vacancies may be filled for the remainder of the year in which they may happen, by the said board of directors, or a majority of them; and in case of the absence of the president, the said board of directors, or a majority of them, may appoint a president pro tempore, who shall have such power and functions as the by-laws of the said corporation shall provide.

Election of directors.

Vacancies.

Not void for failure to elect

4. *And be it enacted*, That in case it shall happen that an election of directors should not be made during the day when, pursuant to this act, it ought to be made, the said corporation shall not for that cause be deemed to be dissolved, but such election may be held at any other time, in the manner provided by law in such cases; and the directors for the time

being shall continue to hold their office until others shall have been chosen in their places.

5. *And be it enacted*, That five directors of the said corporation shall be competent to transact all business of said corporation, and shall have power to call in the capital stock of said company, by such installments, and at such times, as they may direct; and in case of the non-payment of said installments, or any one of them, to forfeit the share or shares upon which such default shall arise; *provided*, that no such installment shall exceed five dollars per share, and that no two installments shall be required within twenty days of each other. Duty of directors. Proviso.

6. *And be it enacted*, That the president and directors of the said company be and they are hereby authorized and invested with all the rights and powers necessary and expedient to survey, lay out, and construct a railroad from the borough of Pemberton, in the county of Burlington, to the borough of Hightstown, in the county of Mercer, connecting at Pemberton with the terminus of the Burlington County Railroad, and at or near Hightstown with the Camden and Amboy Railroad, and passing en route through or near the villages of Wrightstown and Cookstown, in Burlington county, the villages of New Egypt and Hornerstown, in Ocean county, and of Fillmore and Imlaystown, in Monmouth county; *provided always*, that the said railroad shall not exceed one hundred feet in width, except in such places where, from the depth of the excavation or the height of the embankment, it is necessary to take more land for the slope and protection of the side banks of said railroad, in which case so much land as will be necessary for the purpose, and no more, shall be taken, with as many sets of tracks and rails as the company may deem necessary. Powers and objects. Route of road. Proviso.

7. *And be it enacted*, That it shall and may be lawful for the president and directors of said company, their agents, engineers, superintendents, or others in their employ, to enter at all times upon all lands and waters, for the purpose of exploring, surveying, leveling, or laying out the said route of May enter on lands, &c.

such railroad, and of locating the same, and to make and erect all necessary works, buildings and appendages thereof, doing no unnecessary injury to private or other property; and when the route of such road shall have been determined upon, and a survey of such route deposited in the office of the secretary of state, then it shall be lawful for the said company, by its officers, agents, engineers, superintendents, contractors, workmen, and other persons in their employ, to enter upon, take possession of, hold, have, use, occupy, and excavate any such lands, and to erect embankments, bridges, and all other works necessary to lay rails, and to do all other things which shall be suitable or necessary for the completion or repair of the said road, subject to such compensation as is hereinafter provided; *provided always*, that the payment, or tender of the payment, of all damages for the occupancy of lands through which the said railroad may be laid out be made before the said company, or any person under their direction or employ, shall enter upon or break ground in the premises, except for the purpose of surveying or laying out said road, unless the consent of the owner or owners of such land be first had and obtained.

Proviso.

Proceedings when company and owners cannot agree.

8. *And be it enacted*, That when the said company, or its agents, cannot agree with the owner or owners of such required lands for the use or purchase thereof, or if, by reason of the legal incapacity or absence of such owner or owners, no such agreement can be made, a particular description of the land so required for the use of the said company, in the construction of said road, shall be given in writing, under the oath or affirmation of some engineer or proper agent of the company, and also the name or names of the occupant or occupants, if any there be, and of the owner or owners, if known, and their residence, if the same can be ascertained, to one of the justices of the supreme court of this state, who shall cause the said company to give notice thereof to the persons interested, if known and in this state, or if unknown or out of this state to make publication thereof as he shall direct, for any term not less than twenty days, and to assign a particular

time and place for the appointment of the commissioners hereinafter named; at which time, upon satisfactory evidence to him of the service or publication of such notice aforesaid, he shall appoint, under his hand and seal, three disinterested and judicious freeholders, residents in the county in which the lands in controversy lie, commissioners to examine and appraise the said lands, and to assess the damages, upon such notice, not less than twenty days, to be given to the persons interested, as shall be directed by the justice making such appointment; and it shall be the duty of the said commissioners (having first taken an oath or affirmation before some person duly authorized to administer the same, faithfully and impartially to examine the matter in question, and to make a true report, according to the best of their skill and understanding,) to meet at the time and place appointed, and to proceed to view and examine the said lands, and to make a just and equitable estimate or appraisement of the value of the same, and assessment of damages which shall be paid by the company for such land and damages aforesaid; and the said commissioners are also directed and required to assess the damages which any individual or individuals may sustain by the said road, arising from the removing the fencing on the line of the route of said road, through any improved lands over which the same may run; which report shall be made in writing, under the hands and seals of the said commissioners, or any two of them, and filed within ten days' thereafter, together with the aforesaid description of the land, and the appointment and oaths and affirmations aforesaid, in the clerk's office of said supreme court, to remain of record therein; which report, or a copy thereof, certified by the clerk of said court, shall at all times be considered as plenary evidence of the right of said company to have, hold, use, occupy, possess and enjoy the said land, or of the said owner or owners to recover the amount of said valuation, with interest and costs, in an action of debt, in any court of competent jurisdiction, in a suit to be instituted against the company, if they shall neglect or refuse to pay the same for twenty days' after demand made of their treasurer, and shall, from time to time, constitute a lien upon the property of the company, in the nature of a mortgage; and the said justice of the supreme court shall, upon application of either party, and on reasonable notice to the others, tax and allow such costs, fees and expenses to the said justice, commissioners, clerks, and other persons performing any of the duties prescribed in this section, as they or he shall think equitable and right, which shall be paid by the company; *provided always*, that should the said company, or the owner or owners of any of the land or materials, feel himself, herself, or themselves aggrieved by the decision of the commissioners aforesaid, he, she or they may appeal to the next circuit court of the county wherein the said lands or materials may lie.

Proviso.

Parties may appeal.

9. *And be it enacted*, That every appeal from the decision of commissioners appointed under the preceding section shall be made in writing, and in the form of petition to said court, and filed with the clerk of said circuit court of the county wherein the lands or materials appraised by the said commissioners shall be, and notice in writing of such appeal shall be given to the opposite party within ten days after the filing thereof, which proceeding shall vest in said circuit court full right and power to hear and adjudge the same, and to direct a proper issue for the trial of the said controversy to be formed between the said parties, and to order a jury to be struck, and a view of the premises to be had, and the said issue to be tried at the next term of said court to be holden in said county, upon the like notice, and in the same manner, as other issues in the said court are tried; and it shall be the duty of the said jury to assess the value of the said land and damages sustained, and if they shall find a greater sum than the said commissioners shall have awarded in favor of the said owner or owners, then judgment thereon, with costs, shall be entered against the said company, and execution awarded therefor; but if the said jury shall be applied for by the owner or owners, and shall find a less sum than the said company shall have offered or the said commissioners awarded, then said

costs to be paid by said applicant or applicants, and either deducted out of the said sum found by the said jury, or execution awarded therefor, as the said court shall direct, but such application shall not prevent the company from taking the said land upon filing the aforesaid report; *provided*, that in no case whatever shall the said company enter upon or take possession of any lands of any person or persons for the purpose of actually constructing said railroad, or of making any erections or improvements whatever, or otherwise appropriating said lands to the use of said company until they have paid to the party or parties entitled to receive the same, the amount assessed by the said commissioners as the value of such lands and damages, in case the report of the commissioners is not appealed from, then the amount which shall be found by the jury by whom the issue shall be tried; but in case the party or parties entitled to receive the amount assessed by the commissioners, in case there shall be no appeal found by the jury, and in case of an appeal shall refuse, upon tender thereof being made, to receive the same, or shall be out of the state, or under any legal disability, then the payment of the amount assessed or found as aforesaid into the circuit court of the county where the said lands lie shall be deemed a legal and valid payment; and further, that the party or parties entitled to receive the amount assessed by the commissioners, may, upon tender thereof being made, receive the same, without being barred thereby from his, her or their appeal from the report of the commissioners. Proviso.

10. *And be it enacted*, That it shall be the duty of said company to construct and keep in repair good and sufficient bridges or passages over or under the said railroad, where any public or other road, now or hereafter laid out, shall cross the same, so that the passage of carriages, horses and cattle on the said road shall not be materially impeded thereby, and also where the said road shall intersect any farm or lands of any individual, to provide and keep in repair suitable and convenient wagon-ways over or under said railroad. To construct and repair bridges.

11. *And be it enacted*, That the president and directors of

May purchase and run engines and cars. the said company shall have power to have constructed, or to purchase with the funds of the company, and to place on the said railroad, all machinery, engines, cars, wagons, carriages or vehicles, for the transportation of persons or any species of property, as they may think reasonable, expedient or right; and they are hereby authorized to demand and receive such sum or sums of money for transportation of persons and every species of property whatsoever thereon, as they, from time to time, shall think reasonable and proper; *provided*, that they shall not charge more than at the rate of four cents per mile for carrying each passenger; but no charge shall be required to be less in the aggregate than ten cents, nor shall said company charge more than eight cents per ton per mile for the transportation of every species of property on said road, in the carriages of said company.

Proviso.

May hold real estate.

12. *And be it enacted*, That the said company may purchase, have and hold real estate at the commencement and terminus of their railroad, and at any intermediate depot upon the line of the same, not exceeding six acres at each place, and may erect and build thereon houses, warehouses, stables, machine shops, and such other buildings and improvements as they may deem expedient for the safety of property, and the construction of carriages, and other necessary uses, and take and receive the rents, profits and emoluments thereof; and shall have the privilege and authority to erect, build and maintain over such creeks or streams as the said railroad may cross, such piers, bridges, and other facilities as they may think expedient and necessary for the full enjoyment of all the benefits conferred by this act.

Dividends.

13. *And be it enacted*, That the president and directors of the said company shall declare and make such dividends as they may deem prudent and proper, from time to time, out of the net profits of the said railroad, and pay the same to the stockholders of the said company, or to their legal representatives, in proportion to the number of shares held by them respectively.

14. *And be it enacted*, That it shall be lawful for the said

company, at any time during the continuance of its charter, to make such contracts and engagements with any other corporation, or with individuals, for transporting or conveying any kind of goods, produce, merchandise, freight, or passengers, and to enforce the fulfillment of such contracts. May make contracts.

15. *And be it enacted*, That if any person shall wilfully impair, injure, destroy, or obstruct the use of the railroad, or any part of said railroad, enjoyed under the provisions of this act, or of any of the necessary works, wharves, bridges, carriages or machines of the said corporation, such person or persons so offending shall forfeit and pay to the said company the sum of fifty dollars, to be by them recovered in any court having competent jurisdiction, in an action of debt, and further, shall be liable for all damages. Penalty for injuring works.

16. *And be it enacted*, That when five miles or more of said road shall be completed the said company may commence running cars for the transportation of passengers and freight, enjoying all the privileges and subject to the restrictions created by this act. When to commence.

17. *And be it enacted*, That as soon as the said railroad, with its appendages, shall be finished so as to be used, the president and treasurer of said company shall file, under oath or affirmation, a statement of the amount of the costs of said road, including all expenses, and the amount of all purchases made by virtue of this act, in the office of the secretary of state of this state, and, annually thereafter, the president and treasurer of the said company shall, under oath or affirmation, make a statement to the legislature of this state of the proceeds of said road; and from and after the said railroad, or any part thereof, shall be in operation, the said corporation shall pay to the treasurer of this state a tax of one-half of one per centum on the capital stock of said road, to be paid annually thereafter, on the first Monday in January of each year, and such other state tax as may be assessed from time to time by a general law, applicable to all railroads over which the legislature shall have power for that purpose at the time of the passage of such law or laws. Statement to be filed. State tax to be paid.

May borrow money.

18. *And be it enacted*, That the said corporation shall have power to borrow such sum or sums of money, from time to time, as shall be necessary to build, construct or repair said road, and furnish the said corporation with all the necessary engines and machinery for the uses and objects of said company, and to secure the payment thereof by bond or mortgage, or otherwise, on the said road, lands, privileges, franchises and appurtenances of or belonging to said corporation, at a rate of interest not exceeding seven per centum per annum; *provided*, that it shall not be lawful for the said company to plead any statute or statutes of this state against usury in any suit in law or equity, instituted to enforce the payment of any bond or mortgage executed under this section.

Proviso.

State may take road at valuation.

19. *And be it enacted*, That at any time after the expiration of thirty years from the completion of said road, the legislature of this state may cause an appraisement of the said road, with the appendages thereof, to be made by six persons, three of whom shall be appointed by the chief justice of the state for the time being, the remaining three by the said company, who, or a majority of them, shall report the value thereof to the legislature within one year from the time of their appointment; or if they cannot agree, they shall choose a seventh, who, or a majority of them, shall report as aforesaid; or in case the said company shall neglect or refuse to appoint the said three persons, on their part, for two months' after notice of the said appointment by the said chief justice, then the said three persons so appointed by him shall proceed to make such appraisement, which shall be binding on the said company; or in case the said six commissioners shall be appointed as aforesaid, and cannot agree upon the seventh man, then, upon two weeks' notice to the said company, the said chief justice shall appoint such seventh man as aforesaid, and thereupon the state shall have the privilege for two years, of taking said road, upon payment to the company of the amount of said appraisement within one year after electing to take said road; which report shall be filed in the office of

the secretary of state, and the whole property and interest of the said road, and the appendages thereof, shall be vested in the state of New Jersey, upon the payment to the said company of the amount so reported; *provided*, that the said valuation shall in no case exceed the first cost of the said road, with the appendages thereof. Proviso.

20. *And be it enacted*, That if the said railroad shall not be commenced within three years, and completed within six years, from the fourth day of July next ensuing, that then and in that case this act shall be void. Limitation.

21. *And be it enacted*, That the governor, the chancellor, the justices of the supreme court, the attorney general, and the judges of the court of errors of this state, when traveling for the purpose of discharging the duties of their offices, and the members of both houses of the legislature of this state, during their annual or other sessions, shall pass and repass on the railroad of said company, in their cars, free of charge. Who to ride free.

Approved March 24, 1864.

AGREEMENT.

Agreement made the thirtieth day of November, A. D. 1865, *between the Delaware and Raritan Canal and Camden and Amboy Railroad and Transportation Companies, party of the first part, and the Commissioners named in the Act of the Legislature of New Jersey incorporating the Pemberton and Hightstown Railroad Company, approved March* 24, 1864, *party of the second part.*

If the said Commissioners, or the Pemberton and Hightstown Railroad Company, will construct and complete, ready for use, their railroad from Pemberton to Hightstown, as hereinafter mentioned, including two locomotives, three passenger cars and eight freight cars, then the party of the first part hereby agree to lease the same from the time of its completion, during the continuance of the charters of the respective companies, paying therefor, in equal semi-annual payments, on the first days of January and July in each year, the interest, at the rate of six per centum per annum on the cost thereof; (A) *provided*, that the said railroad shall be constructed under the direction, and according to the location and plans, of the Engineer of the Camden and Amboy Railroad, and that the contracts, purchases and expenditures, except those pertaining to the right of way, shall be made by him, and all paid for in cash, and not in stock or bonds; *and also provided*, that the land for said railroad, free of all incumbrances, sixty-six feet wide or more, when necessary for cuts or fills, and earth for embankments, and land free of incumbrances for depot purposes, to be selected by said engineer, not exceeding three acres at each station, and the damages, and the fencing, all of which fencing shall be maintained by the adjacent land-holders, shall not altogether be computed, in ascertaining the amount to be paid under the lease, to have cost more than fifty thousand dollars; *and provided also*, that no incumbrance shall be placed on the said railroad unless the same shall be subsequent to, and subject to, the lease, and then the interest thereon may be paid by the party of the first part, and the amount so paid deducted from the rent hereinbefore agreed upon; *and provided also*, that the party of the first part may, at their option, purchase the said railroad at any time, either before or during said lease, at the cost determined as hereinbefore mentioned, paying the stockholders therefor according to their respective interests.

The party of the second part agree, that, after procuring the necessary authority, they, or the board of directors succeeding them, shall execute a formal lease to the party of the first part, on the terms hereinbefore mentioned

The party of the first part, at every election, shall have the appointment of three directors.

On the expiration of the lease, rolling stock, of equal value to that which shall be placed on the road as above agreed upon, shall be left on the same by the party of the first part.

In witness whereof, the said party of the first part have caused their corporate seals to be hereunto affixed, and their Presidents have hereunto subscribed their names, and the party of the second part have hereunto set their hands and seals, the day and year first above written.

(A.)—The interest on the expenditures during the time that the completion of the work may be delayed for want of funds, or by legal impediments, or by any fault of the party of the second part, or the Pemberton and Hightstown Railroad Company, shall not be added to the cost.

R. F. STOCKTON, *President*, [Corporate Seal.]
E. A. STEVENS, *President*, [Corporate Seal.]
GEO. F. FORT, [SEAL.]
SAMUEL STOCKTON, [SEAL.]

COLLIN B. MEIRS, [SEAL.]
N. S. RUE, [SEAL.]
JAMES S. GIBERSON, [SEAL.]
HARRISON G. WRIGHT, [SEAL.]
JOS. K. HULME, [SEAL.]
RICHARD H. CONOVER, [SEAL.]
JOB H. GASKILL, [SEAL.]
RICHARD WALN, [SEAL.]
GILBERT S. LAWRIE, [SEAL.]
JOHN S. IRICK, [SEAL.]

Signed, sealed and delivered in presence of

The last paragraph, marked A, to be taken as a continuation of the paragraph on the first page ending with "cost thereof."

As to party of the first part, RICHARD F. STEVENS.

Witness as to party of second part, A. J. SMITH.

ROBERT RUSLING, *Witness to John S. Irick signing.*

PRINCETON, NEW JERSEY, December 11th, 1865.

To the Commissioners of the Pemberton and Hightstown R. R. Co.:

GENTLEMEN:—At a meeting of the Executive Committee of the Delaware and Raritan Canal and the Camden and Amboy Railroad and Transportation Companies, it was this day ordered that the agreement with you be amended in the following notes explanatory:—The lessees agree to pay all national and state taxes on the corporation and their property and on the business of the road, but not the tax on dividends.

At the expiration of the lease the property to be delivered up in as good order and repair as when received, improvements made by the lessees being taken into consideration.

The expenses of maintaining the organization and incidental expenses, not exceeding five hundred dollars per annum, to be paid by the lessees.

A true copy of minutes.

RICHARD STOCKTON,
Secretary of Executive Committee of D. & R. Canal and C. & A. R. R. & Transportation Companies.

The undersigned, Commissioners of the Pemberton and Hightstown Railroad Company, do hereby agree to the within named amendments to the original agreement.

Witness our hands, this third day of January, A. D. 1866.

GEO. F. FORT,
SAM'L STOCKTON,
COLLIN B. MEIRS,
N. S. RUE,
JAMES S. GIBERSON,
HARRISON G. WRIGHT,
JOS. K. HULME,
JOB H. GASKILL,
RICHARD WALN,
RICHARD H. CONOVER,
JOHN S. IRICK,
GILBERT S. LAWRIE.

AN ACT to ratify an agreement made between the Delaware and Raritan Canal and Camden and Amboy Railroad and Transportation Companies of the one part, and the Commissioners of the Pemberton and Hightstown Railroad Company of the other part.

WHEREAS, by an agreement made the thirteenth day of November, Anno Domini eighteen hundred and sixty-five, between the Delaware and Raritan Canal and Camden and Amboy Railroad and Transportation Companies, party of the first part, and the commissioners named in the act entitled "An Act to incorporate the Pemberton and Hightstown Railroad Company," approved March twenty-fourth, eighteen hundred and sixty-four, party of the second part, it is provided that if the said Commissioners or the Pemberton and Hightstown Railroad Company will construct and equip, ready for use, as in the said agreement specified, their railroad from Pemberton to Hightstown, then and in that case the said party of the first part will lease the same during the continuance of the charter of the respective companies, upon the terms and conditions set forth in said agreement; and whereas the legal confirmation of the said agreement will encourage the subscription to the stock of the said Pemberton and Hightstown Railroad Company, and give satisfaction to those interested in the construction of said railroad—therefore,

1. BE IT ENACTED *by the Senate and General Assembly of the State of New Jersey*, That the power and authority of the said the Delaware and Raritan Canal and Camden and Amboy Railroad and Transportation Companies and the said Commissioners of the Pemberton and Hightstown Railroad Company, to make such agreement, is hereby declared, recognized and affirmed, and that any lease or leases, contract or contracts, now made, or which may be hereafter made, entered into, or executed in pursuance of such agreement, are hereby declared, and the same shall be, to all intents and purposes, legal and valid; *provided*, that the said lease or leases, and contract or contracts, and the said agreement shall not be held to grant any other power, privilege or right not granted to said companies respectively by their charters and the supplements thereto.

2. *And be it enacted,* That it shall and may be lawful for the Delaware and Raritan Canal and Camden and Amboy Railroad and Transportation Companies to purchase of the said Pemberton and Hightstown Railroad Company their railroad and its appurtenances, at any time as may be agreed upon between the said companies, according to the terms of said agreement.

3. *And be it enacted,* That in case it shall become necessary for the Pemberton and Hightstown Railroad Company to borrow money, as empowered by the eighteenth section of the act incorporating said company, it shall and may be lawful for the Delaware and Raritan Canal and Camden and Amboy Railroad and Transportation Companies, in furtherance of the objects of said agreement, to guarantee the payment of moneys so borrowed, by endorsing the bonds or other negotiable paper of said Pemberton and Hightstown Railroad Company.

4. *And be it enacted,* That in furtherance of the objects of said agreement, it shall and may be lawful for the Delaware and Raritan Canal and Camden and Amboy Railroad and Transportation Companies, and they are hereby authorized, to subscribe for and take any number of shares not exceeding one-half of the capital stock of the said Pemberton and Hightstown Railroad Company.

Approved February 5, 1866.

MORTGAGE.

THIS INDENTURE, made this first day of July, in the year of our Lord one thousand eight hundred and sixty-seven, between "The Pemberton and Hightstown Railroad Company," a corporation under the laws of the State of New Jersey, of the first part, and Mahlon Hutchinson and John S. Irick, Esquires, of the County of Burlington, and State aforesaid, and Ezra Bowen, Esquire, of the City of Philadelphia, and State of Pennsylvania, of the second part:

Whereas "The Pemberton and Hightstown Railroad Company," by their charter, are authorized to "construct a railroad from the borough of Pemberton, in the county of Burlington, to the borough of Hightstown, in the county of Mercer, connecting at Pemberton with the terminus of the Burlington County Railroad, and at or near Hightstown with the Camden and Amboy Railroad, and passing, en route, through or near the villages of Wrightstown and Cookstown, in Burlington county, the villages of New Egypt and Hornerstown, in Ocean county, and of Fillmore and Imlaystown, in Monmouth county," and for that purpose have power to borrow money, at interest not exceeding seven per centum per annum, on bond or otherwise, and to secure the payment thereof by a mortgage upon the property, road, lands, privileges, franchises and appurtenances of or belonging to said corporation; and whereas, at a meeting of the Board of Directors of the said party hereto of the first part, duly convened and held at the City of Bordentown on the twenty-seventh day of June, in the year of our Lord one thousand eight hundred and sixty-seven, after reciting, by way of preamble, that, for the purpose of completing the construction of the railroad from the borough of Pemberton to the borough of Hightstown, it is deemed necessary and expedient to borrow the sum of one hundred and sixty thousand dollars, to be secured by a mortgage on their railroad, lands, privileges, franchises and appurtenances, it was, in substance and effect, "*Resolved*, that the said party of the first part should make and issue their bonds to the aggregate amount of one hundred and sixty thousand dollars, one hundred of which should be for one thousand dollars each, one hundred of which should be for five hundred dollars each, and one hundred of them for one hundred dollars each; and that they all should bear date on the first day of July, in the year of our Lord one thousand eight hundred and sixty-seven, and be made payable on the first day of July, in the year of our Lord one thousand eight hundred and eighty-nine, and should bear interest from their date, at the rate of seven per centum per annum, payable semi-annually, on the first days of January and July of each year during that period, and that for such interest, coupons should be attached to said bonds; that to secure the payment of the said bonds the said party of the first part should make, and in due form of law, acknowledge or prove, and deliver to the said Mahlon Hutchinson, John S. Irick and Ezra Bowen, as mortgagees in trust, their Indenture of Mortgage on their railroad as located and authorized, from the borough of Pemberton, in the county of Burlington, to the borough of Hightstown, in the county of Mercer, aforesaid, and as the same might be hereafter located and constructed between the termini aforesaid, with the appendages, together with the lands of said road, and all such other property appertaining thereto, as they should thereafter acquire, and all their corporate rights, liberties, privileges and franchises, with all and singular the appurtenances, except such lands as said company might acquire, and which should not be necessary to retain for railroad purposes; and that said mortgage should be in such form, and with such covenants and provisions, as counsel should advise to be proper and effect its object; that each of said bonds should be numbered, consecutively, from one to three hundred, inclusive, that those of the denomination of one thousand dollars (omitting the name of the payee and the number and the coupons attached,) should each be in the following form, viz:

Loan of $160,000.

$1000. United States of America. No. —.

State of New Jersey.

Bond of " The Pemberton and Hightstown Railroad Company," for One Thousand Dollars, secured by First Mortgage.

"The Pemberton and Hightstown Railroad Company" acknowledge themselves to be indebted in the sum of One Thousand Dollars, lawful money of the United States of America, to be paid to the said ——— or ——— executors, administrators or assigns, at the office of the said Company, in Wrightstown, in the County of Burlington, and State of New Jersey, on the first day of July, A. D. eighteen hundred and eighty-nine, with interest thereon at the rate of seven per centum per annum, payable semi-annually, on the first days of the months of January and July in each year during said period, at their office aforesaid, or at such place or places in the cities of New York or Philadelphia as said Company shall designate, on the delivery of the annexed coupons therefor as they shall respectively become due.

The holder of this bond is entitled to the security to be derived from a mortgage bearing even date herewith, executed by said Company, on their railroad from the borough of Pemberton, in the county of Burlington, to the borough of Hightstown, in the county of Mercer, and State aforesaid, and its appendages, with the lands and depots, and on their corporate rights, privileges, liberties and franchises, and the tolls, incomes and profits thereof, with the appurtenances, (except such lands as said Company have or may acquire, and which shall not be necessary to retain for railroad purposes,) to Mahlon Hutchinson, John S. Irick and Ezra Bowen, in trust, to secure the payment of the principal and interest of three hundred bonds of like import with this, all similar to this, except that the others are for five hundred and one hundred dollars each, amounting in the aggregate to one hundred and sixty thousand dollars, which includes all the mortgage indebtedness of the said Company.

In witness whereof, the said Company have caused these presents to be sealed with their common seal, and to be subscribed by [L. S.] their President and attested by their Secretary, this first day of July, in the year of our Lord one thousand eight hundred and sixty-seven.

——— ———, *President.*

Attest, ——— ———, *Secretary.*

[Revenue Stamp on Mortgage.]

That those bonds of the denomination of five hundred and one hundred dollars should be each in the like form, except so far as that amount should require an alteration in their form; that the President and Secretary should, as soon as conveniently might be thereafter, have the said mortgage prepared and submitted to said Board for adoption and execution, as by reference to the minutes of said Board will more fully and at large appear:

And whereas, the said President and Secretary of said Company, at a subsequent meeting of said Board of Directors, held at the city of Bordentown on the twenty-first day of August, in the year of our Lord one thousand eight hundred and sixty-seven, did report and submit to said Board the said bonds, in the form and of the tenor and effect set forth in the said resolutions, with blanks therein for the names of the respective payees, without number, but with coupons attached; and did also report and submit to said Board this Indenture of Mortgage, (the same and the said bonds being then unexecuted); and thereupon the said Board, by resolution, thereby did approve of and adopt the same and said bonds as in due form, and did order and direct the President of the said party of the first part to execute this Indenture of Mortgage, by affixing hereto the common seal of the said party of the first part, and subscribing his name as such President, and their Secretary to attest such execution, by subscribing his name also hereto as such Secretary, and then delivering the same to the said party of the second part as the voluntary act and deed of the said party of the first part for securing the payment of said bonds as they might be issued, and, having been then executed, either to acknowledge such execution, or else have the same duly proved before a proper officer, and a proper certificate of such acknowledgment or proof written thereon, to the end that the same might be duly recorded in the proper offices, for the effectual security of said bonds as aforesaid; and did also further order and direct their said President and Secretary, from time to time, as the said bonds should be required in the making of said loan of one hundred and sixty thousand dollars, after having numbered the same, and filled up the blanks therein with the name or names of the payees, as contemplated by the resolution first above mentioned, in like manner to execute each of said bonds, and deliver them to the respective payees thereof, to whom and as issued, as by further reference to the minutes of said Board will more fully and at large appear:

Now this Indenture witnesseth, that the said party of the first part, as well for and in consideration of the premises, and for the better securing the payment of said three hundred bonds, amounting to the sum of one hundred and sixty thousand dollars, or so many thereof as have been or shall be issued, with interest thereon, at the said several times appointed for the payment thereof, as of the sum of one dollar, lawful money of the United States of America, unto them well and truly paid by the said party of the second part, at and before the sealing and delivery hereof, the receipt whereof is hereby acknowledged, have granted, bargained, sold, aliened, enfeoffed, released, conveyed, confirmed, assigned, and set over, and by these presents do grant, bargain, sell, alien, enfeoff, release, confirm, assign, and set over, unto the said party of the second part, and to the survivor and survivors of them, their and his heirs, executors, administrators, successors and assigns, all the aforesaid railroad of them, the said party of the first part, as the same is now located and constructed as aforesaid, from the borough of Pemberton, in the county of Burlington, to the borough of Hightstown, in the said county of Mercer, and as the same is or may hereafter be located and constructed between said termini thereof, and the lands, depots, stations, turn-outs, connections, rails, wharves, piers, bridges, warehouses, machine shops, and other buildings and appendages now appertaining to said railroad, and that shall or may hereafter appertain thereto; and also, all the machines, implements and tools of every kind and description, as well those now owned by the said party of the first part and appertaining and belonging to said railroad and its appendages, as those which may hereafter be procured by them for the use of said railroad, and appertain thereto; and also, all the corporate rights, liberties, privileges and franchises of the said party of the first part of and concerning said railroad and the appendages, or in anywise relating thereto, and all the fares, freights, tolls, dividends, incomes, issues and profits that shall or may be in any wise accrue from the said property and franchises, together with, all and singular, the ways, rights, liberties, privileges, waters, water courses, hereditaments and premises thereunto belonging or in anywise appertaining, and the reversion and reversions, remainder and remainders, rents, issues and profits thereof, and all the estate, right, title, interest, property, possession, claim and demand, in law or equity, of them, the said party of the first part, to all and singular the property aforesaid, and every part and parcel thereof, (except such lands as said company have or may acquire, and which shall not be necessary for railroad purposes): to have and to hold the same, with all and singular, the appurtenances unto the said party of the second part, and the survivors and survivor of them, their and his heirs, executors, administrators, successors and assigns forever; but in trust, nevertheless, for the security, equal use and benefit of the several persons to whom the said bonds have been or may be issued, or who shall become the lawful holders thereof, their respective executors, administrators and assigns, according to law, without priority or preference to the holder or holders of any of said bonds, but subject, however, until default shall be made in the payment of the interest or principal of said bonds, as hereinafter mentioned, to permit and suffer the said party of the first part, their successors, lessees and assigns, and their President, Directors, and other officers and agents, to have and retain the free and uninterrupted use, possession, control and management of the said railroad, estate and property hereby granted and assigned or mentioned, or intended so to be, to and for their own proper use, benefit and behoof, the same as if this Indenture had not been made. And the said party of the first part, for themselves and their successors and assigns, have covenanted and agreed, and by these presents do covenant and agree with the said party of the second part, and the survivors and survivor of them, their and his heirs, executors, administrators, successors and assigns, that they, the said party of the first part, their successors and assigns, shall and will pay, or cause to be paid, to the several holders of said bonds, and every of them, their and each of their executors, administrators or assigns, the said principal sums thereof, respectively, on the aforesaid day, and at the place appointed for re-payment thereof; and also all the interest thereon, respectively, on the several days and times, and in the manner therein appointed for the payment thereof, according to the true intent and meaning of said bonds and every of them: Now if, after the said principal sum of said bonds shall have become due and payable, the same, or any part thereof, shall remain unpaid and unsatisfied for the period of three calendar months next after the aforesaid time appointed for the payment thereof, and after demand of payment, then it shall be the duty of the said party of the second part, and the survivors and survivor of them, their and his heirs, executors, administrators and assigns, at the request, in writing, of the holders af said bonds to the amount of fifty thousand dollars of the principal thereof, to enter upon and take possession of the said railroad and its appendages, and all other the estates and property hereby granted or assigned or mentioned, or intended so to be, with the appurtenances, and work, conduct, manage, use, occupy and control the same, and take and receive the rents, issues, incomes and profits thereof, and apply the net proceeds thereof in the same way as hereinafter provided for the application of the net proceeds of the sale of said premises, or else without entering upon or taking possession cf said premises as aforesaid, the said party of the second part, and the survivors and survivor of them, their and his heirs, executors, administrators, successors and assigns, shall, on like written request of the said holders of said bonds to the amount of fifty thousand dollars above specified, proceed, under and by virtue of this Indenture, and the powers and authority hereby conferred on them, to make sale of the said railroad and appendages, and all other the estate and property granted and assigned or mentioned, or intended so to be, and the said corporate rights, liberties, privileges and franchises at public sale, in such way, and on such terms, and at such place or places as they shall deem best for the interest of the holders of said bonds, first giving at least two months' public notice thereof by advertisements, setting forth the time and place of such sale, published at least weekly in at least two of the newspapers printed and published in each of the cities of New York, Trenton and Philadelphia, and in the town of Mount Holly, in the county of Burlington, and shall apply the whole net proceeds of any and all such sales, from time to time, as realized, to the payment, in the first place, of all arrears of interest on said bonds, respectively, in full, and, in the second place, to the payment and discharge of the principal of said bonds in full, if the residue be sufficient for that purpose, but if not, then to distribute and appropriate the same to and among the holders of said bonds in the ratio of the principal sum of the bond or bonds held by them respectively, without priority or preference, retaining, however, always, so much of said net proceeds as may be sufficient to meet the expenses of this trust, and to indemnify the said party of the second part, and the survivors and survivor of them, their and his executors, administrators, successors and assigns, for or against any liabilities, loss or damage that shall or may occur to them in the execution of this trust; and if there should be any surplus, after paying the whole of the interest and principal of said bonds and retaining sufficient for said indemnity, then the said party of the second part, and the survivors and survivor of them, their heirs and his heirs, executors, administrators, successors and assigns, shall pay the same to the said party of the first part, their successors or assigns, and shall re-convey and re-assign all or any of the premises hereby conveyed and assigned, not sold or disposed of as aforesaid; and the said party of the first part, for themselves and their successors and assigns, have further covenanted and agreed, and by these presents do further covenant and agree, with the said party of the second part, and the survivors and survivor of them, their and his heirs, executors, administrators, successors and assigns, that if the place or office of any or either of them, as trustees as aforesaid, shall become vacant by death, resignation, or otherwise, the said party of the first part, their successors and assigns, shall and may, at their option, appoint a new trustee or trustees to fill such vacancies, and such newly appointed trustee or trustees shall take, have, hold, and possess the same estates and powers, and be subject to the same restrictions, limitations, liabilities and conditions, and none other, as the person or persons, trustee or trustees, to fill whose vacant place or places, office or offices, he or they may have been thus appointed; and if need be, or if counsel learned in the law shall so advise, the survivors or survivor of the said party of the second part, their heirs, or his heirs, executors, administrators, successors or assigns, continuing and being trustee or trustees as aforesaid, shall grant, convey and assign to such newly appointed trustee or trustees such estates in the said mortgaged premises as shall or may be necessary to vest in and confer on him or them the estates and powers, and subject him and them to the restrictions, limitations and conditions above mentioned and intended for them to take, have, hold and possess, and be subject to as aforesaid. And the said party of the first part, for themselves and their successors and assigns, have further covenanted and agreed, and by these presents do further covenant and agree, with the said party of the second part, and the successors and successor of them, their and his heirs, executors, administrators, successors and assigns, that they, the said party of the second part, and the survivors and survivor of them, their and his heirs, executors, administrators, successors and assigns, by an acceptance of the estates, powers and trusts hereby vested in and conferred on them or mentioned, and intended so to be, shall incur no liability whatever by reason of the permitting or suffering the said party of the first part, their successors and assigns, to have, retain and control, manage or enjoy the above mentioned mortgaged premises, or any part thereof, nor shall they be liable or responsible for any destruction, deterioration, injury, damage, sale, assignment or transfer that may occur, done or made of or to the same, nor shall they be liable or responsible for or by reason of any loss or damage that shall or may arise by reason of a breach by or on the part of the said party of the first part, their successors or assigns, of any of the covenants herein contained, nor shall they be liable or responsible for any other matter, cause, or thing, except severally and not jointly, each for his own willful and intentional breach or breaches of the trusts herein and hereby expressly vested in or conferred on them or him; and it is hereby understood, covenanted and agreed, by and for all parties that are, shall or may become interested in said trusts, that it is on such express covenants and conditions of exemption from liability or responsibility, that the said party of the second part accepts the said trusts: Provided always, nevertheless, that if the said party of the first part, their successors and assigns, shall and do well and truly pay, or cause to be paid, to the several and respective holders of said bonds, the principal and interest thereof, on the several days and times therein appointed for the payment thereof, according to the true intent and meaning thereof, without any fraud or further delay, that then, and from thenceforth, as well this present Indenture, and all the estates and property hereby granted, conveyed or assigned, and the several bonds, shall cease, determine, and become null and void, anything herein contained to the contrary notwithstanding.

In witness whereof, the said party of the first part have caused these presents to be sealed with their common seal, and to be subscribed by their President and attested by their Secretary, on the day and year first above written.

N. S. RUE,
Pres't P. & H. R. R. Co.
GEO. F. FORT,
Secretary Pem. & Hightstown R. R. Co.

[Seal of Pemberton and Hightstown Railroad Co.]

Signed, sealed and delivered in the presence of

J. W. ALLEN, R. D. KEEN.

[U. S. Revenue Stamp, (cancelled) $160.00.]

State of New Jersey, County of Burlington, ss.:

Be it remembered, that on the twenty-first day of August, in the year of our Lord one thousand eight hundred and sixty-seven, before me, Garrit S. Cannon, one of the Masters of the Court of Chancery of said State, personally appeared Reynold D. Keen, of Bordentown, in the County of Burlington, and State of New Jersey, who, being of full age and by me duly sworn according to law, on his solemn oath did depose and say, that he, the said Reynold D. Keen, is well acquainted with the common seal of "The Pemberton and Hightstown Railroad Company," the grantors mentioned in the above Indenture of Mortgage, and knows that the seal affixed thereto is said common seal; that he, this deponent, was present at the time of the execution thereof, and saw Nathaniel S. Rue, the President of said Company, set the said common seal and subscribe his name thereto as such President, and George F. Fort, the Secretary of said Company, attest the same, by subscribing his name thereto as such Secretary; and that thereupon the said Nathaniel S. Rue, as President as aforesaid, delivered the same to Mahlon Hutchinson, John S. Irick and Ezra Bowen, the grantees therein mentioned, as the voluntary act and deed of the said "The Pemberton and Hightstown Railroad Company;" and that at or immediately after the said execution of said Indenture of Mortgage, he, the said Reynold D. Keen, subscribed his name thereto as a witness thereof, and at the same time James W. Allen also subscribed his name thereto as a witness.

All of which is certified.

GARRIT S. CANNON,
Master in Chancery of New Jersey.

We accept of the trusts conferred on and reposed in us by the within Indenture of Mortgage, according to the covenants and conditions therein contained.

M. HUTCHINSON,
JNO. S. IRICK,
EZRA BOWEN,
Trustees.

[U. S. Revenue Stamp, 5 Cents.]

The payment of the principal and interest of the bonds secured by the above mortgage is also guaranteed by the Delaware and Raritan Canal, the Camden and Amboy Railroad and Transportation, and the New Jersey Railroad and Transportation Companies, by a certificate duly executed on the back of each bond.

GEO. F. FORT, *Secretary.*

www.ingramcontent.com/pod-product-compliance
Lightning Source LLC
LaVergne TN
LVHW011124110826
845150LV00008B/2249

* 9 7 8 1 4 1 8 1 9 5 5 3 3 *